UNDERGROUND WORLDS

UNDERGROUND CITIES

Sonya Newland

CRABTREE
PUBLISHING COMPANY
WWW.CRABTREEBOOKS.COM

CRABTREE
PUBLISHING COMPANY
WWW.CRABTREEBOOKS.COM

Author: Sonya Newland

Editorial Director: Kathy Middleton

Editor: Petrice Custance

Proofreaders: Lorna Notsch, Ellen Rodger

Designer: Steve Mead

Cover design: Tammy McGarr

Production coordinator and
   Prepress technician: Tammy McGarr

Print coordinator: Katherine Berti

Produced for Crabtree Publishing Company
by White-Thomson Publishing Ltd

Photographs

Cover: Shutterstock: ©Beautiful landscape (left), ©Andriy Blokhin
(bottom right); Wikimedia: (top right)

Interior: Alamy: 8 (Rik Hamilton), 9 (adp-images), 14 (Jesse Alexander),
15 (Jesse Alexander), 18 (Hemis), 19 (Hemis), 20 (Lucas Vallecillos), 26–27
(Richard Levine); Julian Baker: 7, 24–25, 27; Getty Images: 10 (ullstein
bild Dtl.), 11 (ullstein bild Dtl.), 12 (Steffi Loos), 12–13 (Steffi Loos), 21
(Bloomberg), 29 (Bloomberg); iStock: 16–17 (ablokhin), 23 (anouchka), 25
(anouchka); Shutterstock: 4–5 (Nina Lishchuk), 5 (Kristi Blokhin), 6
(graphia), 17 (Kiev.Viktor), 22–23 (Sean Pavone), 28 (Amith Nag).

Library and Archives Canada Cataloguing in Publication

Newland, Sonya, author
     Underground cities / Sonya Newland.

(Underground worlds)
Includes index.
Issued in print and electronic formats.
ISBN 978-0-7787-6080-1 (hardcover).--
ISBN 978-0-7787-6162-4 (softcover).--
ISBN 978-1-4271-2249-0 (HTML)

     1. Underground areas--Juvenile literature. 2. Underground
architecture--Juvenile literature. 3. Cities and towns--Juvenile literature.
I. Title.

TA712.N49 2018   j307.76   C2018-905526-X
                                                          C2018-905527-8

Library of Congress Cataloging-in-Publication Data

Names: Newland, Sonya, author.
Title: Underground cities / Sonya Newland.
Description: New York, New York : Crabtree Publishing, 2019. |
     Series: Underground worlds | Includes index.
Identifiers: LCCN 2018043797 (print) | LCCN 2018045854 (ebook) |
     ISBN 9781427122490 (Electronic) |
     ISBN 9780778760801 (hardcover) |
     ISBN 9780778761624 (pbk.)
Subjects: LCSH: Underground areas--Juvenile literature. | Underground
     architecture--Juvenile literature. | Cities and towns--Juvenile literature.
Classification: LCC TA712 (ebook) | LCC TA712 .N48 2019 (print) |
     DDC 307.76--dc23
LC record available at https://lccn.loc.gov/2018043797

Crabtree Publishing Company
www.crabtreebooks.com   1-800-387-7650

Printed in the U.S.A./122018/CG20181005

Published in Canada
Crabtree Publishing
616 Welland Ave.
St. Catharines, Ontario
L2M 5V6

Published in the United States
Crabtree Publishing
PMB 59051
350 Fifth Avenue, 59th Floor
New York, New York 10118

Published in the United Kingdom
Crabtree Publishing
Maritime House
Basin Road North, Hove
BN41 1WR

Published in Australia
Crabtree Publishing
3 Charles Street
Coburg North
VIC, 3058

CONTENTS

UNDERGROUND LIVING

Walk around any city and what do you see? Apartments, offices, and hotels? Shops, restaurants, and recreation areas? Roads and railways? Now imagine if all the things you see around you also existed beneath your feet...

Refuge Underground

In the past, people fled to underground spaces in times of danger. Secret rooms and tunnels beneath ancient castles provided an escape if a fortress fell. Underground shelters kept citizens safe from bombing raids in times of war.

These places might have started out small—perhaps just a room or two—but often they were expanded and equipped for longer-term living. Some grew to become whole towns underground, with sleeping spaces, hospitals, and even entertainment venues.

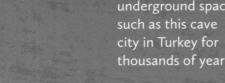

People have lived ▷ and worked in underground spaces such as this cave city in Turkey for thousands of years.

Environmental Issues

More recently, people have started to worry about the effects that growing cities have on the environment. Pollution from cars and factories is causing **climate change**. As cities spread, farmland and countryside are lost. One solution to these problems is to build down instead of out. Designers and **engineers** have found clever ways to construct whole cities underground, including housing, businesses, and transportation systems.

△ There are more than 2,000 shops in the underground part of the city of Montreal.

DID YOU KNOW?

Beneath Cappadocia in Turkey lies what may be the oldest underground city in the world. The homes, churches, temples, and tombs there were built more than 5,000 years ago.

WIELICZKA SALT MINE

Salt was discovered at Wieliczka in Poland in the 1200s. The mine shafts dug to reach the salt were the first of many. Now this huge underground complex includes 186 miles (300 km) of tunnels over nine levels.

Keep Digging

The **medieval** mine shafts did not need to be very deep. As the salt near the surface was used up, however, workers started to dig farther down to find more. To begin with, they worked by hand, using picks and shovels. Later, machinery began to be used in mining. For example, in the 1700s, **treadmills** were introduced—machines that hauled salt to the surface. In 1861, **steel** tracks were laid so that wagons could carry salt and other materials through the mine.

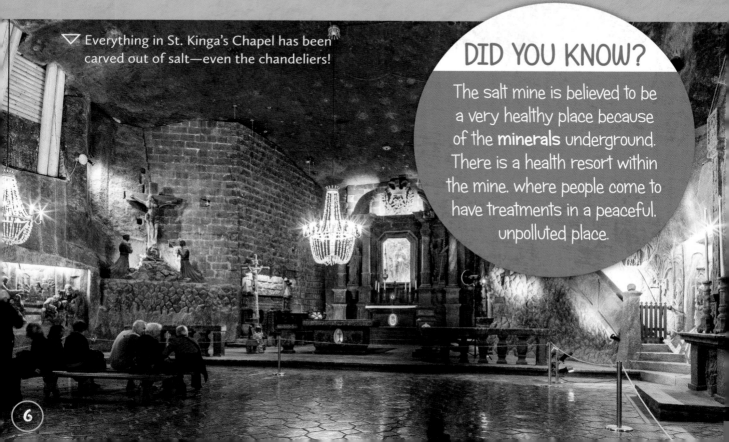

▽ Everything in St. Kinga's Chapel has been carved out of salt—even the chandeliers!

DID YOU KNOW?

The salt mine is believed to be a very healthy place because of the **minerals** underground. There is a health resort within the mine. where people come to have treatments in a peaceful. unpolluted place.

6

Chapels and Chambers

Some of the chambers in Wieliczka are used for mining. But alongside these are rooms that were carved out for other purposes. Mining was a dark, dirty, and dangerous job, and the miners were comforted by religion. There are four underground chapels here, and many other religious monuments such as statues.

Salt was produced on the site up until 2007. But even before the mine fully closed for business, it opened to the public. Every year, more than one million people visit Wieliczka to admire the incredible underground art and architecture.

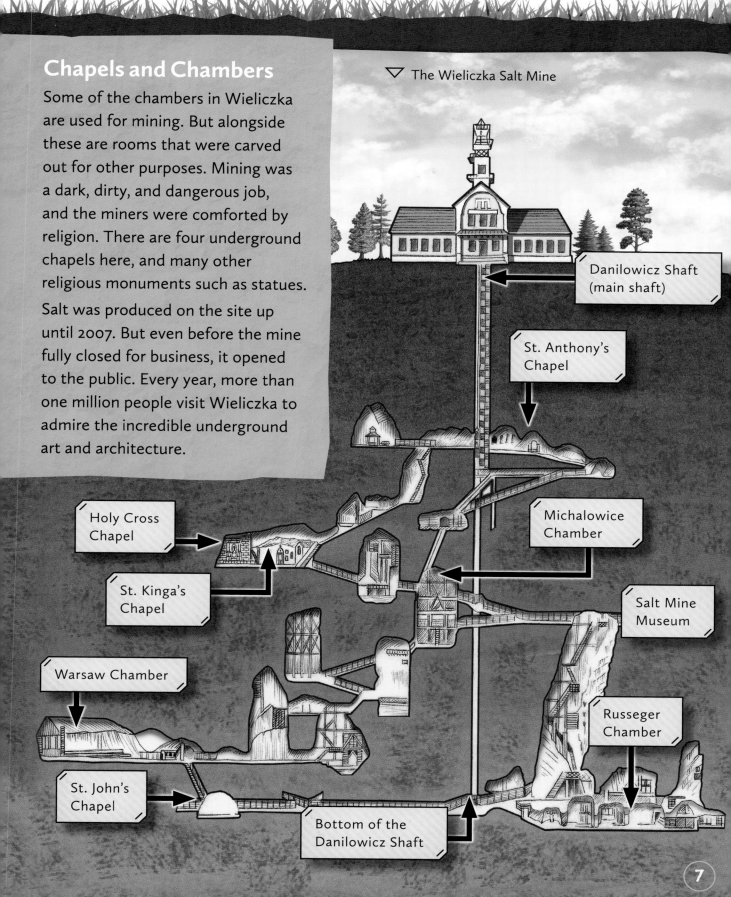

▽ The Wieliczka Salt Mine

Danilowicz Shaft (main shaft)

St. Anthony's Chapel

Holy Cross Chapel

Michalowice Chamber

St. Kinga's Chapel

Salt Mine Museum

Warsaw Chamber

Russeger Chamber

St. John's Chapel

Bottom of the Danilowicz Shaft

UNDERGROUND EDINBURGH

The city of Edinburgh in Scotland has a long tradition of underground living. This began after 1513, when the English defeated the Scots in the Battle of Flodden.

Stop Right There!

Edinburgh was the capital of Scotland, so it was important to keep it safe from enemy armies. A huge wall, known as the Flodden Wall, was built after the battle to enclose and protect the city. As the population continued to grow, more space was needed, but the wall stopped the city from expanding. The people of Edinburgh found a simple solution— they began to build down. Many houses already had cellars and underground storage areas. These were soon turned into **habitable** spaces, and people began living and working underground.

This is a wine storage ▷ area in the South Bridge Vaults.

The South Bridge Vaults

In the 1700s, there were many advances in engineering. Large bridges were built across roads and hills. Whole towns sprang up under the bridges in a network of **concealed** rooms. Edinburgh's South Bridge was completed in 1788, and the **vaults** beneath it soon became known as a city within the city. Lots of businesses opened there, including shops and inns. People crowded into these small, windowless spaces.

△ Today, displays in the vaults are designed to scare visitors during tours of Edinburgh's underground city.

DID YOU KNOW?

Burke and Hare were two **notorious** Scottish murderers who killed 16 people in 1828. They are said to have hidden the bodies in the South Bridge Vaults before selling them to a doctor for research.

BERLIN BUNKERS

Beneath the German capital of Berlin is one of the biggest underground complexes in the world. Created in the years before **World War II**, this extraordinary city is a maze of now-abandoned tunnels and **bunkers**.

Hitler's Vision

The German leader in the 1930s was Adolf Hitler. Hitler wanted to destroy anyone he believed was Germany's enemy and to create a great future for his country. Part of his vision was to transform Berlin into a city that would show off Germany's strength and power to the world. Hitler asked his architect, Albert Speer, to create designs for a new city. Hitler planned to call it "Germania."

◁ This is a scale model of Speer's plan for "Germania." Only one structure was ever completed—a huge sports stadium.

▽ Tunnels were built to house a new, fast rail link that would connect different parts of the city.

Speer's Plans

Speer dreamed up a new capital built around a long road called the "Avenue of Splendors." There would be wide, open spaces and magnificent buildings. The reorganization would not only take place aboveground. Speer's plan included a new transportation system built beneath the city. This would enable people to travel quickly and efficiently. There would be a whole system of underground roads and train tracks. Workers began digging the tunnels in 1937, but two years later, war broke out. Suddenly the tunnels were put to another use—as bomb shelters.

Underground Bunkers

Throughout the war, British, **Commonwealth**, French, and American air forces dropped bombs on the German capital. During these air raids, the people of Berlin would seek safety in the tunnels beneath the streets. Rooms were added to the underground network so that people could sleep and eat more comfortably. Some of these chambers had steel doors to protect people in case the enemy launched a poisonous gas attack. Arrows were marked on the walls to help people find their way around the underground city.

△ This bunker could sleep nine people in hammocks along the walls.

The Tunnels Today

By the end of the war in 1945, Germany was defeated and Hitler was dead. His vision for Berlin was never realized, and the tunnels were not used. Today, however, they are considered an important part of German history.

There are organized tours to these "Berliner Unterwelten," which means Berlin underworlds. Only part of the complex is open to the public, but visitors can explore some of the underground bunkers and passages.

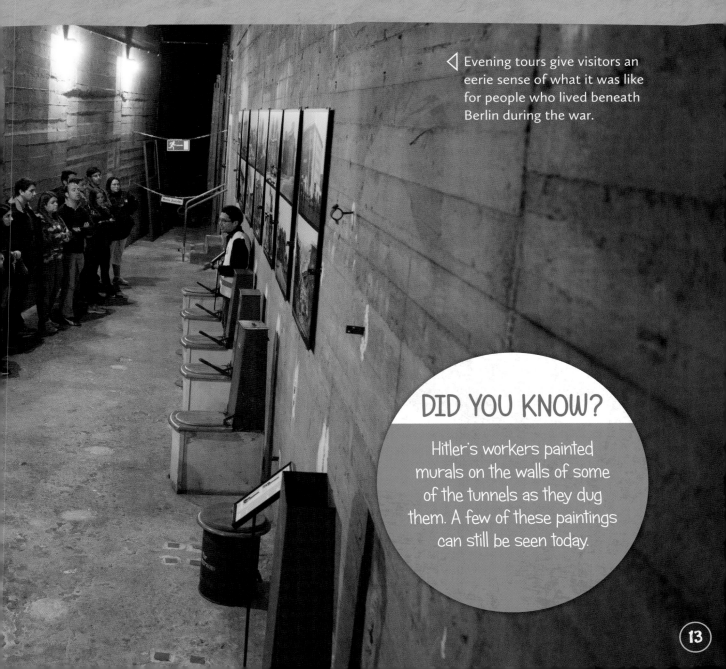

◁ Evening tours give visitors an eerie sense of what it was like for people who lived beneath Berlin during the war.

DID YOU KNOW?

Hitler's workers painted murals on the walls of some of the tunnels as they dug them. A few of these paintings can still be seen today.

BURLINGTON BUNKER

Toward the end of World War II, scientists developed **nuclear weapons**. People around the world were afraid of what would happen if a nuclear attack took place. The only way to survive would be to hide underground.

Protecting the Leader

If a nuclear attack took place, it would be important for a country's leader and government to stay safe. In the United States, an underground bunker was built beneath the White House to protect the president. In England, near the town of Corsham, a stone quarry was considered the perfect place for an underground escape for the prime minister. Work began on the bunker in 1955. It was so secret that it was given a codename—"Burlington."

▽ The telephone switchboard in the Burlington bunker is one of the largest of its kind in the world.

Underground Town

It was estimated that up to 4,000 people might have to use the bunker, so it was designed with many **facilities**. There was a hospital, a train station, two cafeterias, and even a water treatment plant. A BBC radio station was installed so that broadcasts could be made from underground. Electric carts were provided to help people get around. In total, the site covered 60 miles (95 km).

DID YOU KNOW?

British government members would be safe in Burlington, but they weren't allowed to bring their families into the bunker!

△ Workrooms were equipped with beds, desks, and typewriters so government staff could continue working while underground.

Coming in From the Cold

For 40 years, the government kept everything in the bunker in working order, just in case they needed it. They never did. When the **Cold War** ended in 1991, the bunker was **decommissioned**. Still, it was only in 2004 that the public learned that it existed.

RÉSO, MONTREAL

Montreal in Canada is a city on two levels. Above the ground, apartment blocks, hotels, and offices line the streets. These building are linked by a huge underground network of tunnels and plazas packed with shops, restaurants, and businesses.

DID YOU KNOW?

RÉSO was generally known as the Underground City until 2004. It was renamed to sound like the French word *réseau*, which means "network."

It's Cold Outside

In winter, temperatures in Montreal drop below freezing. The authorities wanted to find a way to beat the cold—and the traffic—in the city. In 1962, while Montreal's first skyscraper, the Place Ville Marie, was being built, city planner Vincent Ponte came up with an idea. Why not build an underground shopping mall nearby so people could shop in the warmth? The mall was joined by a tunnel to the main rail station and a nearby hotel. The underground city of RÉSO had begun...

Shopping malls stretch from underground to aboveground in Montreal.

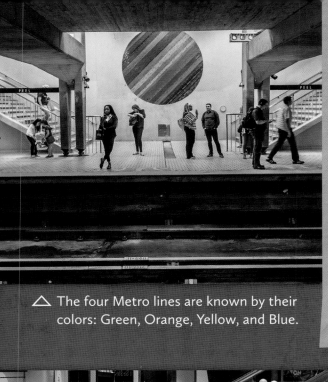

Rapid Transport beneath Your Feet

The next big expansion was building a subway system. The Montreal Metro began as three rail lines linking 26 underground stations. Later, a fourth line was added, and there are now 68 stations on the Metro. Today, people can get around quickly—and without going out in the cold! There are plans to extend the Metro even farther, joining central areas to the outer reaches of the city.

△ The four Metro lines are known by their colors: Green, Orange, Yellow, and Blue.

Niveau Ste-Catherine

Niveau Métro
↓ Niveau Tunnel ↓

Art Underground

This underground city isn't just a place for shopping and business—it's also a cultural center. Stations in the Montreal Metro are famous for their artwork. Other parts of the underground city are also home to many pieces of art. Temporary displays turn the tunnels into art galleries at times, too. An organization called Art Souterrain ("Underground Art") arranges exhibitions of modern art for people to enjoy, and even hosts an annual art festival.

△ A temporary art display, part of an annual exhibition, lines the tunnel walls in the underground city.

DID YOU KNOW?

RÉSO is the largest underground city in the world. More than half a million people use it every day.

Underground History

Traveling down the escalators, at first sight RÉSO looks like a bright, modern shopping complex. But there are 20 miles (32 km) of pedestrian tunnels in underground Montreal, and they hide some history. The edges of an underground vault border one of the tunnels, indicating that a bank once stood above it. And the courtyard of an old hotel is now a shopping mall!

△ People can access the underground city via 120 entrances on the surface, scattered all over Montreal.

DIXIA CHENG

In the 1970s, China grew afraid of a nuclear attack by the Soviet Union. The Chinese leader, Mao Zedong, told his people they should "dig deep tunnels, store food, and prepare for war."

Putting the People to Work

In China's capital, Beijing, people were given shovels and asked to start digging deep tunnels. Engineers from the army told them what to do, but it was ordinary citizens who dug Dixia Cheng, the Chinese term for an underground city. When completed, it covered 33 square miles (85 square km). It could be accessed by nearly 100 secret entrances hidden all over Beijing.

◁ Originally, the tunnel walls were hung with pictures of Mao Zedong and slogans encouraging people to be prepared.

Survival Strategies

There was enough space, equipment, and supplies in Dixia Cheng for 300,000 people to live safely for up to four months, if needed. Around 10,000 bunkers were dug out for families to live in. There were schools, a hospital, cinemas, factories, and even an ice rink! A ventilation system replaced stale air inside with fresh air from the surface.

A New Underground Community

Thankfully, Dixia Cheng was never needed as a **refuge** from attack. But in recent years, it has become a refuge of a different kind. Beijing is a crowded city. When people move there in search of work or students come to study, they often have nowhere to live. Even though the bunkers are not official shelters, around a million people are thought to be crowded into them every night.

DID YOU KNOW?

Dixia Cheng was so big it was nicknamed the "Underground Great Wall," after the famous Great Wall of China, which was once 13,000 miles (21,000 km) long!

▽ Some people have set up shops in the bunkers under Beijing.

UNDERGROUND CITY, HELSINKI

Finland is one of the most environmentally friendly countries in the world. It has the best record for using renewable energy sources. The "underground city" beneath the capital, Helsinki, helps with this in several ways.

Saving Space

The spread of cities aboveground causes pollution and other environmental problems. So, when more space was needed in Helsinki, planners looked down rather than out. Instead of sitting on soil, Helsinki is built on solid **bedrock**. The authorities realized they could dig into this rock and carve out useful spaces. The rock is a natural insulator, keeping heat in. So an added advantage is that anything built underground needs less energy for heating.

The underground ▷ Temppeliaukio Church is also known as the "Church of the Rock."

DID YOU KNOW?

A huge swimming hall covers two levels underground. It is so big that 1,000 people can swim there at a time.

Underground Eyesores

A lot of the underground facilities are things that people do not want to see aboveground. For example, there is a coal storage facility in this "shadow city," as it is sometimes known. This means that coal heaps do not spoil the beauty of the landscape above. That space might be freed up soon, as the Finnish government hopes to ban the use of coal by 2030. There are facilities for the public too, though. The underground city includes a shopping area, a hockey rink, a church, and parking spaces.

△ Like many underground cities, Helsinki's includes shopping areas and subway stations.

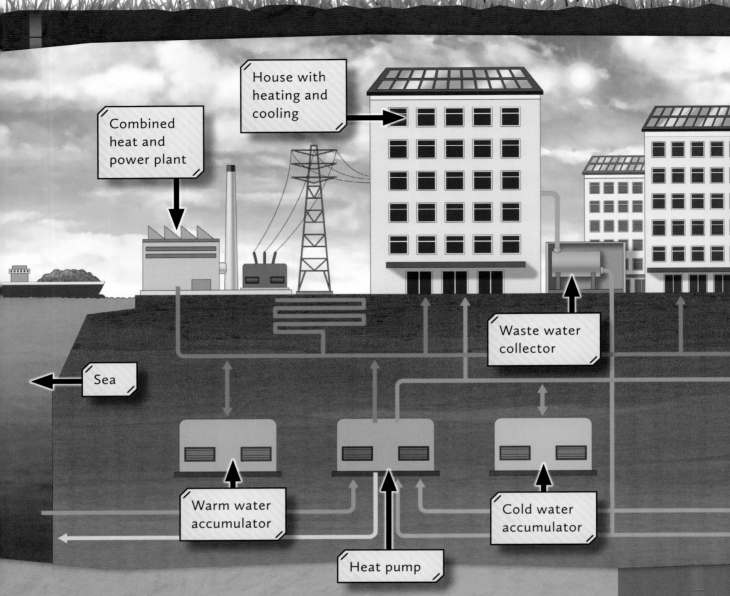

Combined heat and power plant

House with heating and cooling

Sea

Waste water collector

Warm water accumulator

Cold water accumulator

Heat pump

Cooling Machines

One of the most important features of the underground city is the data center. A data center is where a business focuses its technology, so it contains a lot of computers and other machines. Helsinki's data center lies 100 feet (30 m) underground, but it is unusual in another way, too. The machines are kept cool using seawater circulated by underground pipes. The heat from the computers is channeled back to the surface. There it is used in the aboveground city's heating system. This cuts energy costs and is better for the environment.

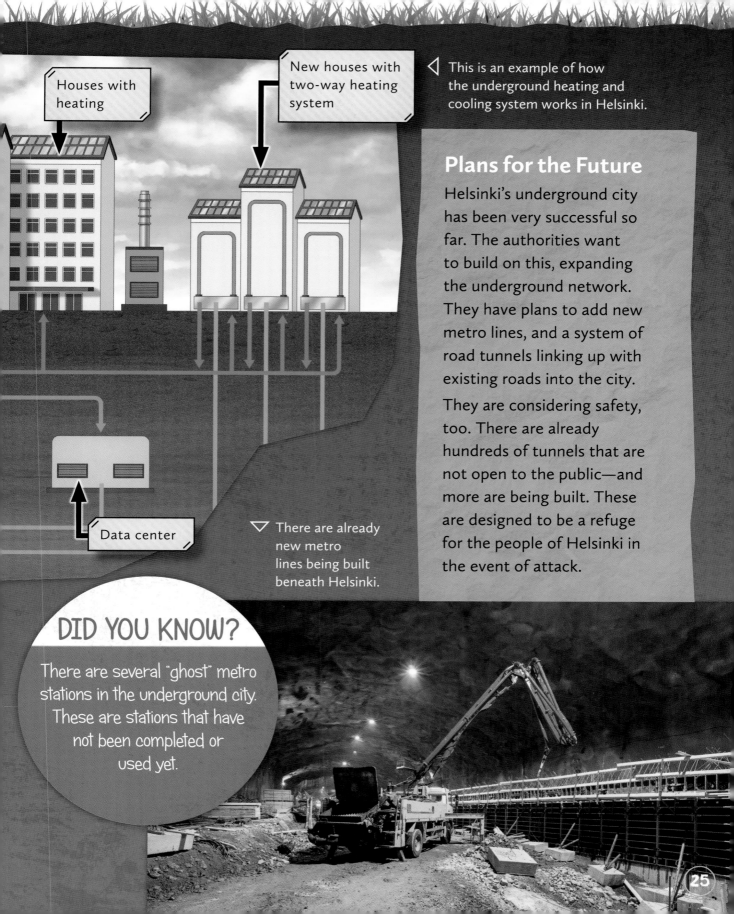

Houses with heating

New houses with two-way heating system

◁ This is an example of how the underground heating and cooling system works in Helsinki.

Data center

▽ There are already new metro lines being built beneath Helsinki.

Plans for the Future

Helsinki's underground city has been very successful so far. The authorities want to build on this, expanding the underground network. They have plans to add new metro lines, and a system of road tunnels linking up with existing roads into the city.

They are considering safety, too. There are already hundreds of tunnels that are not open to the public—and more are being built. These are designed to be a refuge for the people of Helsinki in the event of attack.

DID YOU KNOW?

There are several "ghost" metro stations in the underground city. These are stations that have not been completed or used yet.

THE LOWLINE

In 2012, James Ramsey and Dan Barasch had an idea. They wanted to turn an abandoned trolley park in Manhattan into a real park. But this would be a park with a difference. It would be completely underground.

Kickstarting the Park

They launched the project on Kickstarter—a way of raising money from the public. More than 3,300 people liked the idea, giving $150,000 to get it off the ground. The next step was trying out a **prototype**. This "Lowline Lab" was an indoor version of the park, set up to test the technology. More than 3,000 plants of 70 different **species** were grown in the lab. It opened to the public in 2015.

26

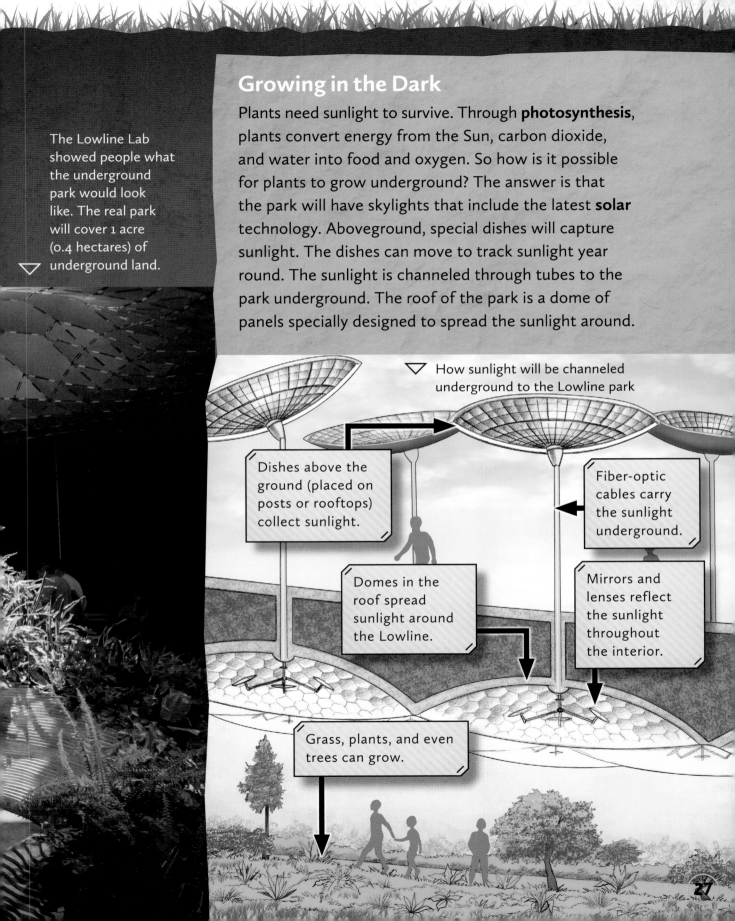

The Lowline Lab showed people what the underground park would look like. The real park will cover 1 acre (0.4 hectares) of underground land.

Growing in the Dark

Plants need sunlight to survive. Through **photosynthesis**, plants convert energy from the Sun, carbon dioxide, and water into food and oxygen. So how is it possible for plants to grow underground? The answer is that the park will have skylights that include the latest **solar** technology. Aboveground, special dishes will capture sunlight. The dishes can move to track sunlight year round. The sunlight is channeled through tubes to the park underground. The roof of the park is a dome of panels specially designed to spread the sunlight around.

▽ How sunlight will be channeled underground to the Lowline park

Dishes above the ground (placed on posts or rooftops) collect sunlight.

Fiber-optic cables carry the sunlight underground.

Domes in the roof spread sunlight around the Lowline.

Mirrors and lenses reflect the sunlight throughout the interior.

Grass, plants, and even trees can grow.

27

UNDERGROUND SINGAPORE

The population of Singapore is growing rapidly. Over the next 15 years, 1.5 million more people may be living there. Planners are looking at ways to use underground spaces to make more room.

Underground Plans

Like many big cities, Singapore has a fast, efficient subway system, which carries more than three million passengers a day. A new rail line is already being built, and two more are planned. There are also underground shopping areas connected by pedestrian tunnels. One suggestion for this growing region is to extend these tunnels to join more parts of the city. More malls, restaurants, and other attractions could then be built underground, as well as **subterranean** bicycle lanes.

◁ Underground walkways are accessed by staircases and escalators all over the city.

A City for Scientists

Another plan is for a 50-acre (20-hectare) underground "science city." This would have 40 connected **caverns** for scientists to work in. The caverns would be data centers, offices, and laboratories for researchers. More than 4,000 people could work in this science city.

The Jurong Rock Caverns

Another big underground project is already underway in Singapore. A storage facility is being built in rock caverns on the nearby island of Jurong. When completed, the facility will store oil and chemicals. It is safer to store these substances underground, as it is cooler, so there is less risk of a deadly fire. The facility will also free up 150 acres (61 hectares) of land aboveground.

DID YOU KNOW?

The Jurong Rock Caverns will eventually have storage space amounting to more than 1,000 Olympic-size swimming pools.

▽ The Jurong caverns are 430 feet (130 m) underground and as tall as a nine-story building.

GLOSSARY

bedrock A layer of solid rock that lies very close to the surface of Earth

bunker An underground shelter built to be very strong to protect against bomb attacks

cavern An underground space like a small cave

climate change The change in regular weather patterns as measured over a number of years

Cold War A period between 1946 and 1991 when the Soviet Union and the U.S. were enemies

Commonwealth A group of colonies and former colonies of Britain including Canada, Australia, New Zealand, and India (known until 1949 as the British Commonwealth)

concealed Hidden away

decommissioned Taken out of military service

engineer A person who designs and builds structures or machines

facilities Equipment or places designed for particular purposes

habitable Describing somewhere people can live comfortably

medieval A period of history from about 500–1450 C.E.

minerals Substances that occur naturally in the earth

notorious Famous for doing something bad

nuclear weapons Very powerful bombs

photosynthesis The process in plants that turns energy from the Sun, carbon dioxide, and water into food

prototype The first version of something, built to see if an idea works

refuge A safe place

solar Describing something that uses the Sun for energy

species A group of plants or animals that share similar features

steel A strong metal made from iron

subterranean Below the ground

treadmill A type of machine powered by humans

vault A large underground room usually used for storage

World War II A global conflict that lasted from 1939 to 1945

LEARNING MORE

Books

Hyde, Natalie. *Ancient Underground Structures.* Crabtree Books, 2018.

Stefoff, Rebecca. *Building Tunnels.* Cavendish Square, 2015.

Rose, Simon. *Underground Transportation Systems.* Crabtree Books, 2018.

Website

https://app.kidslisten.org/ep/But-Why-A-Podcast-for-Curious-Kids-Are-There-Underground-Cities

This fascinating podcast tells you about some of the world's most amazing underground cities, both ancient and modern.

INDEX